D1622880

88 DALE EARNHARDT JR.

Superstars of NASCAR

RIGHT ON!

Michael Ford

Gareth Stevens
Publishing

Please visit our Web site, www.garethstevens.com. For a free color catalog of all our high-quality books, call toll free 1-800-542-2595 or fax 1-877-542-2596.

Library of Congress Cataloging-in-Publication Data

Ford, Michael, 1980-
Dale Earnhardt, Jr. / Michael Ford.
    p. cm. — (Superstars of NASCAR)
Includes index.
 ISBN 978-1-4339-3948-8 (pbk.)
 ISBN 978-1-4339-3949-5 (6-pack)
 ISBN 978-1-4339-3947-1 (library binding)
1. Earnhardt, Dale, Jr.—Juvenile literature. 2. Automobile racing drivers—United States—Biography—Juvenile literature. I. Title.
GV1032.E19F67 2010
796.72092—dc22
[B]

                          2010007740

First Edition

Published in 2011 by
Gareth Stevens Publishing
111 East 14th Street, Suite 349
New York, NY 10003

Copyright © 2011 Gareth Stevens Publishing

Designer: Michael J. Flynn
Editor: Mary Ann Hoffman

Photo credits: Cover (Dale Earnhardt Jr.), p. 1 Rusty Jarrett/Getty Images; cover, pp. 4, 6, 8, 12, 14, 16, 18, 22, 24, 26, 28 (background on all) Shutterstock.com; pp. 5, 10–11 RacingOne/ISC Archives/Getty Images; pp. 7, 9 Dozier Mobley/Getty Images; p. 13 David Taylor/Getty Images; p. 15 Kevin Winter/Getty Images; pp. 17, 20–21 Jonathan Ferrey/Getty Images; p. 19 Kevin Kane/WireImage/Getty Images; p. 23 Chris Graythen/Getty Images; p. 25 Layne Murdoch/Getty Images; p. 27 Jonathan Daniel/Getty Images; p. 29 Jeff Bottari/Getty Images.

Printed in the United States of America

CPSIA compliance information: Batch #CS10GS: For further information contact Gareth Stevens, New York, New York at 1-800-542-2595.

Contents

A Famous Father

Dale Earnhardt Jr. had a famous father. Dale Earnhardt Sr. was a very famous NASCAR driver. He died in 2001.

Dale Earnhardt Sr.

Dale Earnhardt Jr.

Race Car Driver

Dale Earnhardt Jr. was born in North Carolina on October 10, 1974. He wanted to be a race car driver like his father and grandfather. He is sometimes known as "Little E."

Dale Sr.

Dale Jr.

7

Dale Jr. was very interested in race cars. He began racing when he was 17. He went to school to learn how cars work.

Stock Car Racing

Dale Jr. began racing stock cars in national races in 1996. He began racing for his father's team in 1998.

11

Dale Jr. won NASCAR championships in 1998 and 1999. In 2000, Dale raced against his father and stepbrother in a race. It's one of the few times family members were in the same race.

An Author

In 2002, Dale wrote a book about becoming a race car driver. He wrote about the world of NASCAR.

15

Record Breaker

In 2003, Dale broke a record at Talladega Superspeedway. He was the first driver to win four races in a row on that racetrack.

Big Races!

In February 2004, Dale won the Daytona 500. This is the "Super Bowl" of stock car racing!

Dale Earnhardt Jr.

Many people think the Daytona 500 is the most important NASCAR race. It's the first race of the NASCAR Sprint Cup Series season. Daytona Beach is where NASCAR began.

The Coca-Cola 600 race was special in 2007. Dale and other NASCAR stars had their cars repainted for this race. They raced to raise money for military families.

23

New Team, New Number

In 2008, Dale began racing for a different racing team. He felt he would have a better chance of winning races with a new team.

Rick Hendrick

Dale Earnhardt Jr.

Dale drove a race car with the number 8 for many years. When he started with his new team, he drove a car with the number 88.

Dale Earnhardt Jr. has had 40 NASCAR wins. He is one of the most popular drivers in NASCAR.

Timeline

1974 Dale is born in North Carolina.

1998 Dale wins his first NASCAR championship.

2002 Dale writes a book about his life in NASCAR.

2003 Dale breaks a record at Talladega Superspeedway.

2004 Dale wins the Daytona 500.

2008 Dale joins a new racing team and gets a new car number.

For More Information

Books:

Armentrout, David, and Patricia Armentrout. *Dale Earnhardt Jr.* Vero Beach, FL: Rourke Publishing, 2005.

Gigliotti, Jim. *Dale Earnhardt Jr.* Mankato, MN: Child's World, 2009.

Roza, Greg. *Dale Earnhardt Jr.: NASCAR Driver.* New York, NY: Rosen Publishing Group, 2007.

Web Sites:

Dale Earnhardt Jr.
www.dalejr.com

The Dale Earnhardt Jr. Pit Stop
www.dalejrpitstop.com

Glossary

championship: a series of races to decide a winner

military: having to do with the army, navy, or air force

Sprint Cup Series: the top racing series of NASCAR

stock car: a racing car that looks like a regular car

Super Bowl: a championship football game

Talladega Superspeedway: the largest and steepest speedway in NASCAR

Index